ATTITUDES TO SUSSEX

Poems
by Robert Edwards

Illustrated
by Karen Grace

Burble

Also by Robert Edwards:

Brighton Burble
Bridge Bluster
Beech Blurt

Note on references in the text

Blue Idol: *Sussex* by Ian Nairn and Nikolaus Pevsner, in The Buildings of England series published by Penguin Books, 1965

Glyndebourne: *Letters from England* by Robert Southey, originally published under a false name by Longman's in 1807, printed by the Cressnet Press in 1951, edited by Jack Simmons

ISBN 0 9525909 2 1

Copyright © Robert Edwards 2006

First published by Burble in 1995 as Attitude to Sussex

Published by Burble, 12 Marine Square, Brighton, Sussex, BN2 1DL

Printed by One Digital, Brighton, Sussex, England

Printed on recycled material

British Library Cataloguing in Publication Data. A catalogue record for this book is available from the British Library

Robert Edwards was born in Cuckfield in 1950 and lived for eighteen years in Danehill where his Welsh father was the village schoolmaster. His mother, grandmother and great-grandmother were born and lived in Sussex. He did philosophy at York and two postgraduate years at Sheffield. For twelve years he lived in London, returning to Sussex in 1988. He lives in Brighton.

Karen Grace was born in Cuckfield in 1955. She went to Bath Academy of Art, then returned to Sussex. She and her family live in Brighton.

PREFACE TO FIRST EDITION

I would like to thank various people for their help: first, the Fame Frame and the Billy Silver Show at the Zap Club in Brighton for enabling me to dramatise readings of several of these items; Chris Sansom for taking a party of us to Worthing; Lindsay Morris for ornithology; Fifi de Maintenon for leading me around Shoreham; Will Stone for his camera in Bells Yew Green and Brighton; Mr John Blackman and his colleagues at Carmichael's; and finally my thanks to my sister for her artwork - I cannot imagine how she found the time.

PREFACE TO SECOND EDITION

To learn that a revised edition would require a new ISBN number, and would be counted in publication terms as a separate or different book, was rather disconcerting. The title of the 1995 version was Attitude to Sussex. It was never a very comfortable name, so I have taken the opportunity to make a slight alter-ation to the title, as well as to the occasional word or line in the contents. Parts of West Pier Lettering first appeared in the Brighton Burble collection published in 1999. I must again thank John Blackman and colleagues for more than printing. For their interest and encouragement I would also like to thank David Arscott, the Sussex Ramblers Association, the independ-ent booksellers who have sold my books, and the independent readers who have bought them.

R.E.

CONTENTS

Sandstone schools and hammer-pond pools
hedgerow flowers by saxon church towers
gentle ridges by stone river bridges
yew tree hedges and cliff top ledges
muffled-hooting owls and sea gulls' howls
high-sided alleys at seaside valleys
bluebell woods and bees wax goods
low hipped roofs over cart horse hoofs
pebbled walls and tudor halls
black mathematical tiles near bare down miles
pumpkins champion, round blue rampion
palace archaic and ancient mosaic
rushes and reeds and saltmarsh weeds
and sheep and cows under gorse flamed brows
forest deer, regional beer
white wooden posts north of white wavy coasts
half-timbered houses' contented drowses
placid faces in sleepy places
grass-shrouded village name signs
deeply rural railway lines
lone ashlar mansions - indolent scansions
on rock pools, chalk and loam
resolve to laze at home.

JANUARY IN ARUNDEL

The open field, over the way from the railway
Station, upholds a balance - flood water puddled ,
Pooled and channelled - integral to the level.

While the Lavant plays havoc not many miles
From here, here the Arun, abnormally wide
And high, is much contained - cold, milky brown.

Crossing the river road's alley path, a cat
Of some length and bulk, thick persian grey,
Keeps its head and tail low down, intent.

The sun pours light in drops that blink and bounce
On the walled and straightened town centre river.
The river almost fills the bridge's arches.

Three Frenchmen study a pub lunch menu. I
Buy myself a birthday coach-house coffee.
The town is compact, a red and grey rockery.

Dipped in the downs, the valley curve hugs east
Round the ridge end, with a lane lined with cracked
Green-silver trees flecked in bright red buds.

The effect is a constellation of softest
Burgundy, trailing wispy. Above, clean-cut,
The castle breaks clear - like cinema in the sky.

DITCHLING BEACON

In swoop and leaping arc the land
Records the first coast snowfall
In three whole years.

The sun - this morning's cloud-smoked brass -
Has forged an apparition
Rife with ice blue.

Could landscape wear a character
More tranquil? Snow can sprinkle -
Chalkish condiment.

But fresh new forces, frigid, bite.
Gusts, abrupt - twice - chill
The brow's lean flesh.

BLACKDOWN

In the undulating labyrinth matt-mooded
Villages are limberly secluded.

Lurgashall and Lickfold and Fernhurst
Trickle where the copse-drop angles flatten first.

All of a corner intimately seen -
Each is a fringe of a three-cornered green.

Opening like a slowly unclenched palm,
They phrase a familial kind of laid-back charm.

On a February Tuesday the greens are pied
With snow. A snow-capped pub is warm inside.

The publican is genial and polite.
Her voice is cultured, natural and bright.

Out on the road two horse-girls ride with care.
An enthusiastic spaniel takes the air.

On the climb up the downs, a steady flow
Of sleet infiltrates the mist, lit by the snow.

On the densely wooded down the snow's creation
Is a fantastic superdelineation.

Ice-crusted slush is confined to lanes and tracks
Freed by gritters' and timber-tractors' cracks.

Mob-like trees, gangling in their bearing,
Gesticulate in uncompliant sharing.

The name is classic. Black is good. But, crikey.
A more accurate word might surely have been spiky.

OLD TOWN

Embattled but scarcely embittered, Hastings
Was always more hardy than hip -
But history speaks few famouser names
With quite such a sense of zip.

In Ramsgate the boats are more painterly,
And in Teignmouth their sails look swish;
The harbour in Scarborough graces the salt
But in Hastings the beach boats breathe fish.

While Sargassos of eel and Dovers of sole
And Severns of salmon and trout
Trawl custom and clublife, Hastings is home
To what haphazard hunger's about.

No dish was ever more welcome to me
Than chips with fish from Hastings.
For me, the marvel is less in perfection
Than in the long choice of tastings.

The tea shops in Rye may be mecca for many
And film crews should flock to Camber -
As happy as they who modestly stray
To these platefuls of yellow and amber.

NEW TOWN

Saturday shoppers divert from crime
Fears of insulting by framing in rhyme
Strange observation. And life tends to art:
Viz "the motor mart for every part".
Happy the town that is all mundane
If its homogeneity stays humane.

It is hard to imagine, now, the conviction
Of town and country planning. Their precinct
Utopia must live out their commission -
A public risking of more than whisking winds.
Its concourse remains a daring arena -
A nineteen-fifties collectors item, candied
And calendared by mottled mosaic yellow
And sea-green strip. There was a tenderness
In the dream, and hopes, which live on
In the public library, and breathe through
The daffodils, white and yellow, in the yard
Of the old pale gold stone church. The past
Appears peculiarly in the pale grey corner
At Robinson Road on the High Street.

A most-modern mall, commonly narrow -
Purpose-designed so that nothing must harrow
The senses - is less maladroit than many.
But indoor emporia are prim-puff zenny.
And out in the item awaiting re-grading
A war-born utopian clarion is fading.
Bus and train station are squandered, sorely
Pointing how government serves them poorly.
A wholesome arrangement of houses is surely
What comforts those whose home is Crawley.

BLUE IDOL

In an old-fashioned shire guide book
I'd lit upon something bizarre.
The name had been haunting me all day long
Like a far flung Shangri La.

It sounded like a Marlene Dietrich film,
Or an old Roy Orbison song,
Or a long lost childhood library book -
A place where my dreams might belong.

The guide said nothing at all about
The present day use of the place;
And gave little clue to its whereabouts -
What little, I couldn't trace.

A seventeenth century timbered farm,
Then a quakers worship house, then...
To go by the book, it might as well now
Be a waltz by Johann Strauss.

Where must it be? Where could it be?
What was I going to do?
I would not rest until I had seen
This idol washed in blue.

If only an angel would come for me
And lead me by the hand -
I'd willingly depart from reality
For one view of Blue Idol Land.

The most beautiful buildings I ever saw,
The cathedrals - white and gold -
Of the Kremlin - they would be nothing compared
With what I should now behold.

Well, I would not settle for idleness yet:
I was determined to know.
The guide book referred to an intricate code
Revealing where to go.

But when the revelation worked
And the place came into view,
I should be idle as never before
When washed in the sacred blue.

I ran to alternative references.
The phone book was first. The name
Appeared applied to a guest house - playing
The same tantalising game.

Seizing the black and red Pevsner published
In 1965,
It was midnight as the pages were flicked
And I pictured a starlight drive.

The index, improbably, listed the thing
And, on page one hundred and seven,
The fine, lamented Ian Nairn
Confirmed my belief in heaven.

The description was much that one might have hoped
And in one sentence faith was fulfilled:
'This must have been how the Cistercians felt
When they began to build.'

A realisation grew - the above
Was a serious matter to quote.
I nonetheless thirsted on epithets
'Lovely and remote'.

The quakers might never forgive me for gushing
In language so adventitious;
But what else on earth could they really expect
With addresses this delicious?

Two days later, the time has arrived.
The dawn is chill, and dry.
The morning turns mild. Pressure is lowered.
Pale cloud occupies the sky.

The journey is brisk and smooth. Coolham
Is cheerfully brief with suspense.
No signs exist to point the way. It is
Now that the progress is tense.

Finally looms on the left a board -
White, the lettering blue.
I wonder if I will go through with this,
While, magnetically pulled, I do.

The rough lane, lined with unkempt trees
Comes to an oak-clumped halt,
And primroses and periwinkles -
Modest to a fault.

And there - for real - beyond sloping grass,
A sunken, path-bound prize -
It is, to this day, a Friends Meeting House, far
Too devout to idolise.

BADGER AT PULBOROUGH

Late at night on an Easter Monday,
Coming back from the Cotswolds,
Cruising the flexuous erratic undulation,
The car zooms like a camera. Hit
By the headlight, an animal walks
Into the road from a hedge on the right.
The car begins to brake, but the creature
Continues across the road. The waddle
Develops into a trot, but the long body,
Bright in the glare as a log of silver birch,
Possibly yellowish in youthful fur,
Moves deceptively slowly on the short legs.
The car has virtually to pause to let it by.

It looked a clean and careful thing.
I hoped it could be happy
And forget but not forgive me for my car.

BLUEBELL RAILWAY

Halt at a half-crazed open house
Of industry, in the half-awake
Many-sheltered wheeled. Hear ring,
Clatter, clank, hiss and singeing sigh.
Trundle out among the moundy fields,
Banks overhung with fresh
Silky green - paved high blue.

Regarding the carriage as lustrous,
Liveried and clean, passengers best
Recapture each a private bequest -
Warm colours of the cushioned seats,
The shiny profusion of carpentered
Glass and varnished wood -
Detail keeping quaint from counterfeit.

Funny to acquiesce in reverence,
Tributes to the arduous and ardent
Archive, arched in broad-leaf birdlife -
Integrity can be lonely. Cutting
The continual swathe, grazing
Territory where livestock grazes -
All demeanours coalesce. The line's
First history was long, while
The revival is already the length
Of a middle-aged person's life.

Legendary dedication
To locomotion - steam sacrosanct -
Weighs like iron, worship of which
Provides for unpaid privilege
And conveyance to fulfilment.
While movement is primed
For public enrolment,
Authenticity is arbiter, criterion.

Work is done by people
With skills learned from love
And in some - redundant
Or retired - from labour
In real life. The ostentation
Is old and true, and a sadness
Of reality in romance marks
The idea of the whole
Original unlikelihood.

We, who can afford to, will
Subvent by ticket price this costly
Tinkering with forensic travel
Through field and forest space and time. So -
All with wild hyacinth to imbue,
Bell petal melt and bathe us blue.

PEVENSEY TO WADHURST BY TRAIN

Anderida's relic rises grey, refortified
By Norman adaptation. A white calf
Jumps over lumps of pasture. Ponies,
Ruggedly ragged, bow their heads.
Pevensey Levels are laid lower, more
Visible in the train than by road.
On Normans Bay the sea froth seems
Inches from trackside touch. Cooden -
You couldn't but tell. Bare red bricks
Of Bexhill station, sprucely scoured,
Are like a subterranean monastery.
Along by the beach again - a wind-surf
Or wind-sail hurtles to hand, to usher
A hundred white wooden chalets at
St Leonards old west marina.
A magpie flies upward through
Trees under Warrior Square.
All change at Hastings.
After the poppies and thistles and flags
Of West Leonards, the hillocks
Are roughly hewn. Before long
The woodlands close in on the windows,
The green shade wields its wildness
Through the eternal battle for time.
Battle - we must be brave.
Farmland fieldscapes wimple-fold.
At rusted sidings, a sprig of broom
Glimmers. The railways line lands down

In a sleepy marsh river valley -
Robertsbridge to Etchingham.
In the middle of a world of merely green
A moment of orange hung tile occurs,
And a bunch of brown cattle in buttercups.
To the simple, solitary, flat-faced red-brick
Railway building at Wadhurst, the winds
Blow loud and low through the swirling trees
Heavy with rain and burly in summer ambition.

GLYNDEBOURNE REOPENING

In countenance the long red house is more
Studious than studied - mind over matter.
Fame has not put affliction on the face
That tolerates our latest surge to flatter.

The gardens climb along the walls. The gardens
Perform a formal role, before they ramble
By the water. The gardens drift away
Into fields where farm animals amble.

'England seems to be the paradise
Of sheep and cattle.' Thus Don Manuel
Alvarez Espriella, comparison's
Invidious impostor, sulking well.

'Never was a nation so unmusical.
Perhaps the want of leisure may be the cause.'
Then look here, where, though leisure is not wanting,
Effort fabricates opera's fanfared floors.

Contemporary technology and old
Craftsmanship create this culture. One
And three-quarter million bricks are laid
To house acoustics said to be second to none.

Denizens of patronage parade
Companionable as neighbours in a ghetto.
A comic opera's play on English weather
Only wants direction, score, libretto.

Comfortable in some front row seats -
Twelve miles from the sound of the champagne,
From the cool and clouded rugless garden -
We watch the show with cans of Castlemaine.

WAKEHURST PLACE

Competitive chaffinches pounce and flounce coquettish
Round the wooden outdoor cafe tables. Their
Vaudeville wit cramps the style of one thrush
And one wary robin. The pheasant is fixated
On the centre of the table, ignoring them all.
Pungent smells of soil and dampness drift
From moss-webbed trees and shrubs. Away and high
On the sloping open short-cut grass, gangs
Of rooks, black and sleek, occupy the tallest
Trees and prime spaces. A west wind
Suddenly sails through the leaves above
The ravine. The himalayan glade is a wondrous
Depth of birdsong, bees and honeysuckle.
At the bottom, the lakeside path -
Soft sodden woodchip carpet - turns on itself
In a swamp. Half up from the depths,
A squirrel scurries through the crinoline
Of a Japanese cedar. A tubby rabbit,
At the foot of a douglas fir, dozes until,
Disturbed, it leaps and bounces through the thick
High grass. The path through the rocks is real
Wealden, ginger and cappuccino coloured;
And further up in the foxgloves, the trees
- Beech, holly, oak and yew - grow direct
From the stone. Higher still, when the day's
Only opening in the cloud allows
The sun through, heat and light breathe
Into the birches, while the wind refreshes

Their flair. Molly and Wally of Hove - names
Given on a bench - glance the way
To the shelterbelting candidature and - so high,
Such vantage - the sapling roble beeches.
Near by, spreadeagled, a pretty young rook lies dead.

SHELLEY BICENTENARY

He scarcely mentioned Sussex
In the verse, or in all
The furious fired tracts.
Too radical to recall
The travesties of change
From fields that freed the child,
He died too young to delve
In what had once beguiled.
He fell in love with Italy,
Having dropped so hard from favour
The probity of Horsham
Despaired of being braver
On his behalf. No Wordsworth
Who turned prodigal, he,
Though given doting sisters
In a baffled family,
Was desperate to burn
The world into a dream
Unrealisable:
A continuous crazed scheme
Involving wife, child, friends.
Now he is out of fashion -
Off the curriculum -
Grief-stricken passion
Elusive to control.

A brisker lyricism
Never travelled, or
More vain mysticism
Confused. So simple to
Dismiss as dankest vim
A victim's wisdom: so
The lore of Brothers Grimm
Was thought more true than his.
However, in among
The fustian and fey
Are works in which are flung
Accounts of clear cold truth.
While we persist in driving
Children out of idyll
We traumatise the thriving.
He had a volcanic temper
And his play was volatile.
But he was happy until he was twelve
In a sand-clay square mile.
Once histrionic paranoia
And social rank collided,
Arbitration only served
To distance the divided.
They can keep their curriculum
And forget what they've destroyed,
While I will weep at Field Place
And dream against this void.

ERSTWHILE GRAMMAR OF
EAST GRINSTEAD

I may have brought it all upon myself.
That the innocence of children can be
Callous, I do not doubt, or that what
Weighs upon their teens is a prejudice
Their mentors never meant to preach.
But after all - how much I feared
The place, it scarcely seemed to guess.

If it is too late, too lacking valour
To bury a hatchet so feeble and slack
There is little hope for me. Unless
It is better this blame is driven not
To something more serious, or someone -
Deeper seeds of evil retaliation.

It is not as if everyone
Was so bad. Most of the worst
Were locked in a kind of cabal
To represent the town -
Averse to the surroundings.
So many secretive sects, too.
Was it so?

Would he be happier with Haywards Heath?
My people debated and rated it no -
While I thought, I could cut these losses -
The fault is not of northernness,
The child, ejected from the forest dug-out,
Must face the fact of change.

My trust was that there might have been
A converse case - an eleven-year-old
Unlike me but caught in common bond -
Hoisted out of Highbrook, wherever, eager
For East Grinstead, hapless in Haywards Heath.

Daily compensation was the comedy
On the bus journeys - the indelicacy
And daftness of the abhorred horde
Exuding lewd wit and erudition, through
The woods, warrens, heather - animistic.
Cold comfort farms were meat and drink to me.
My friends were other villagers. But
A council household befriended me, and
Miss Coles was kind. Miss Coles was kind.

Leaving it as it had been, I left it be.
Each time I later approached a certain
Turn in the road, my stomach turned -
The eleven-year-old's longing for belonging.
Now, in the children's ward, watching
Nurses working with physical burns, I meet
Hospitality and humility, and am ashamed.

SELSEY

The road
Passes thin sand-gold
Velvet cattle in light green
Meadows; past all the thatch
Of Sidlesham; a huge field of
Unforgettable forget-me-not blue.
The east beach sign of Selsey rusts,
Close to the notice to divers, precautions
To meet the Mixon rocks and the Mulberries.
Lanes jam-packed with jumbled housing
Rally in conflations of lush summer blooms
- Amazingly multi-coloured and sundry.
Off the pale-pebbled west shore, birds
Fluster on the fine-lined dune
- The blue of mid-June above
And around. Island-like,
The cul-de-sacs are
Try-to-buy-land-and-build busy
And thatcherless dizzy.
At Selsey Bill,
A woman sits in a red
Straw hat, and a policeman skims
- Walking it by its handlebars -
A bicycle over the beach.
Back on the road out
Beyond the pond water
Black as glass with sun -

Glanced through the trees
Of the coastal plain: like
A fluke-angled flint, points
Green-shouldered
Chichester Cathedral.

EASTBOURNE

At the high arrival point
The wind attacks the earth.
Every blade of feathered grass
Is blown for all its worth.

Children run around the field -
Heads light as candyfloss.
Below, round trees encrust the slopes
Like gigantic moss.

Down between the trees and sea:
A town of soul and poise.
We cannot tame the Channel,
Only humour it with buoys.

Hearing Bridge's idyll
Achieved with lasting force,
I want to know what sea he had
In mind - this unnamed source.

Along the beaches bathers lounge,
Dismantled of their guard.
Tentative, the elderly
Stroll the promenade.

We board the launch for Beachy Head -
A light, wood, graceful thing.
We smile at spray - both young and old,
Where gracefulness is king.

The hotels form an even line,
Handsome in this view -
White and grey, set against
A sky of quiet blue.

The downs rise fast. The off-white cliffs
Are draped in tapered green;
So different from the sea's jade gloss.
The rocks look near - and mean.

Falling on a shoal, the gulls
Show enviable muscle.
The sea is deserted beyond their crowd -
Their winged and watered hustle.

Above the lighthouse, on the ledge
Stand three tiny figures,
Silhouetted in the sun.
Grim jokes greet their rigours.

We are a cosmopolitan group
Of thirty-one, who share
A sense that life should be more like this
- If only we all knew where.

Later, outside the Terminus,
My Harvey's in my hand -
I listen for the hush of one
Who lived in such a land.

GOODWOOD

Viewed from the Singleton side in a high steep field
Of rich green grass, the buildings peer avidly forth
Over the dip of hiding depth, to woven
Folds of woodland, farmland roaming north.

The 2.30 race is two-and-a-half miles long.
An unfancied horse remains way ahead of the rest,
Until at the brow - and, once they hit the straight -
The trail-blazing runner is plainly far from the best.

The land, here beyond the final peter of track,
Feels remote from where the grandstand patrons are.
Then, when the last few furlongs exact their cost -
From the crowd comes a billowing clamour - a brouhaha.

Both the Gordon Enclosure's entrance, broad and roomy,
And the rooftop terrace view, compel the eye.
Impressions of a racegoers' garden party
Build as vain betting flutters to the sky.

The Sussex Stakes triumphantly delivers
The living equine god that was Zafonic.
But a stewards inquiry sanctions a staggering fiasco,
The celestial colt stricken by malady demonic.

The turf, soft from Tuesday's pounding rain,
Will suit a few. The lungeing limber dash
Cannot be the fleetest, but can't detract
From the rampant trample, plunge, thud and flash.

In the Richmond Stakes, Fumo di Londra flatters
To deceive. Much of this time is passed in ambling
On the undulating lawns, around the champagne
Marquee garden and the frenzied tote-hall gambling.

In the 5.20, the colours of Khalid Abdulla
Come right with Electrify. The day, now less uproarious,
Closes in beaming sunlight. Squiffy and amorous,
The punters have licked the racing world's label of Glorious.

WORTHING STARSEARCH

On one of the hottest days of the year
We have come to Worthing Pier.
The tide is out so far, the sea,
Low, is like blue milky tea.
At seven, the theatre rooms belong
To the elderly singer's high-pitched song.
The rest is almost all our own -
A quiet, empty deco zone.
It may be debatable
Whether our inflatable
Parrot and banana brought
Capture quite the joy we sought.
But once inside the theatre, they
Seem at home - as well they may.
For here are inflatables as far
As the eye can see: there are
Reptiles, hammers, clubs galore -
And only a hint of what's in store.
As the hundreds take their seats,
The lights go down, and Worthing greets
Its talent show as if it were
The chance to redress a lifetime slur.
Twirling glow-sticks bright, insectile,
The house prepares each sweet projectile.
Doleful plastic whistles, horns
And klaxons drone. Worthing scorns,
As a middle-aged Peacehaven man
Croons 'Moon River' as best he can;

Beset by wave upon wave of sound,
'Smoke Gets In Your Eyes' is drowned.
Next, the niece of a Worthing aunt
Tries to be heard, but simply can't.
Fifteen people stand and sway
With newspapers, passing the time of day.
The audience boos - a deafening jeer.
Minority counter-cultures cheer.
A teenager called Camilla appears.
The talent sinks five hundred beers,
And joins along with her Abba track -
An art form conjured out of flak.
The girl attempts to speak to them,
Receiving replies of pure mayhem.
More poignant moment to mark her secession:
The newspapers march past the stage in procession.
A rhythmic man, a "Worthing wonder",
Performs a skiffle number, under
Competition from the crowd
Who stamp and clap and grow more loud.
One man dances cowboy style
Up on his seat beside the aisle.
As the act draws to a close
The hooter and drum sound grows and grows -
Half the audience now on its feet.
Inflatable axes loom. Replete
With a feast of misdemeanour,
Like football supporters from Argentina

The audience relents as a dance troupe cavorts
To a Cilla Black single. It takes all sorts.
At this stage the crowd goes relatively quiet -
Conserving energy for its mid-show riot.
Sensing the interval soon to be,
They heckle a Midhurst girl mercilessly.
A Manchester trio give up as soon
As the crackle is burst from the third balloon.
An Angmering stand-up - a cabbage-chopper -
Provokes from the floor their real show-stopper -
His own act so doggedly unflagging,
The spirit on the floor had just been sagging -
Until on shoulders raised sedate:
Eddie the Eagle is their head of state.
Heir to aggression's every spasm
Comes catalysmic enthusiasm.
The final act - from Portslade -
Sings off-key - a heaven made
Chance for the crowd to discharge its last:
Here is new meaning in the term 'lambast'.
The finale - most macabre of all -
Is a colossal sing-song filling the hall.
Of their anthem 'Delilah' the crowd does not tire,
Prolonging their notes like a half-Welsh choir.
It is a most unlikely sight
For Worthing on a Monday night . . .
Into the warm night air - and here:
The pier's lemon lights - demure - austere.

ARLINGTON TERNSEARCH

Cormorants keep to the off-shore woodwork,
Upright and quiet. Scores of Canada geese
Mill about on land. Swallows and martins
Whiz overhead and rollercoast down.
Floppy lapwings flap and sway to heights.
Lone sandpipers tread the shallow edge.
Wagtails drive low over the water.
A greenshank glides and swiftly skims.
Grey heron wings beat slow and heavy,
Folding to shrug and hunch. On a fence
In fields of high blond grass,
Five whinchats watch. Among the fragments
Of pale rock along the bank, dunlins
Nestle, heads buried sideways.
In the centre of the circle
Of the sun-sparked water, patient
Crested grebes dive at trout. At last,
Two common terns trace the perimeter -
Genius of geometry before the blue sky -
Before an egret dangles angelically above.

PORT OF SHOREHAM

In the east end basin of the eastern lengthy
Flat rectangle of water, flat-backed fish-boats
Dock. Among the winches, sheds and cylinders,
Petroleum and sand stand on the north. South,
Belgian crates, timber Swedish, timber baltiski
Are stacked orderly. Along the eerie length
Of cargo platform spit, grey chips of gravel
Lie in conical heaps. Wheat escapes by wind
From pourings off the quay to moorings. Alone
A yellow Italian container waits in space,
Inscrutable. Near, no lack of lorries raging,
Rolling. Here is an ample vessel declaring
Amsterdam. Amsterdam - waves today, to trade
Away. Past the disempowered power station,
Seaward at the locks, the footway where children
Bump their bicycles over the canal, an old
French fishing boat, angular, is berthed. West
Onward, inward, between the breakwaters, inside
The sea, dredging, the dredger turns. The grey
Stone lighthouse lives, alongside the lifeboat
Station. Out to sea, a tanker's low lights
Peak. The coastguard tower is boarded up. Old
Fort is a free and furry playground, deep, green,
Red and grey. On the old fort road, beach-side
Homes are singular as art nouveau. But Lady Bee:
What bee she? Within the wharves, the dowdy
Cloudy dusk, salt river silt is dark graphic grey.

DECO

Figures in a seascape -
Figured of modernity,
Modelled for a spreescape -
Modulate fraternity.

Tubs of cream or ice cream packs
Diagrammatize, decide
Even keel for decks and backs
Ocean-liner-dandified.

Drifting out of building trials,
Fetching up like coastal couches,
Sifted out of starker styles -
Cream of relaxation crouches.

Linear lido, airport ponder,
De la warring, caffyn scattered,
Only wilt for want of wander -
Only airing schemes unmattered.

A HESITANT PAEAN TO THE SUSSEX OUSE

It is really a very small river for something
That sends ferries daily to France.
It is, after all, about twenty miles long
And its width can't be said to enhance
Its portent. No, it's a modest affair
That will seldom say boo to a goose.
But this isn't Devon - it just wouldn't do
For these waters to dart fast and loose.
You can tell it has less than the self-esteem
Of the Garonne saluting Toulouse,
Or the breadth to make headway of cousin the Medway
- It isn't the sort poets choose.

Like its four shire companions it's also in short
Supply of that great money-spinner
Called heritage. This is no bad thing:
You lose sleep when you're onto a winner.
And what is the virtue of all that chalk
And mud clay with its caramel goos,
If it isn't to turn life into a siesta,
One uninterruptible snooze?
Where easing of oarsmen into canoes
Is for sloth, the river's own views
Lack barges and houseboats, the sound is of moos
Or birdsong. Cars aren't what it woos.

Sprung from the beacons of pineclump and heather,
Twenty ditch tributaries cut pale clay deep
Under the shade of beech, hazel, oak, birch,
Rowan, willow, holly - through their leaf heap
To clearings, from brambles to fern and bracken,
Emerald moss and foxgloves. The stream-heads
Of the forest, its brindle floor, chance to dwindle or
Meet into one to pass fields dipped like beds.

This must be why it can seem further shy,
Sheltered by broad leaves above;
Until it is feted in the gap it created -
It hugs Harvey's brewery with love.
Then it proceeds through the flat lands of reeds
And Virginia Woolf's last haunt -
To waft the swans to the forthcoming bay
And the shock of some ships to flaunt.

FAIRLIGHT GLEN

Like scarves in gale force wind
Green fire-break paths fall
To soft and lethal edges
Of cliffs four hundred feet high.

Chinks in the rain sky
Cast drifting streaks of gold and silver
On the sea, way below.

A kestrel quivers
Wind-whipped above the bell heather.
Everywhere the bracken
Is part-brown, part-green.

Down, distant-seeming
In the glen-trickled bay
The rocks appear to be purple-brown.

After the steep descent
Through the woods' shade,
A tunnel of path, the back of the beach
Is banked with golden boulders.

The block rocks in the sand and
Sea pools now chocolate brown,
Many are clothed in feathery green.

A line of pale yellow-pink
Fuses the horizon. In front,
The sea develops from sandy
To pale green, grey, dark blue.

AUTUMN:
COUNCIL HOUSES AT BELLS YEW GREEN

Had I gone too far, and blundered?
Where I should wish to be I wondered
Lest I unleash my cant on Kent
By Bayham - back to Frant. I went
Past a huddle of houses harking south
Stirring muddled cues that stilled my mouth.
Draped in the landmark low-layered tiles
Rufous as fox fur lidding large window styles
- Rust orange eggs in a nest of gold -
Paprika powder to invest and hold
In trust: why must we wait for more?
This is what local councils are for.
An earlier design both bold and fetching
Proves what juices flow through Fletching,
But the mania for local authorities' rout
May reach our brink at this redoubt.

SHIRLEY COLLINS

In a room above a pub,
Gathered by a folk club,
Chaired, the singers lined the fireplace.

Seated second from the right,
She joked and hosted for the night -
Deadpan, tender; sensitive to pace.

Self-deriding Sussex gang,
They were sturdy when they sang -
Raucous chorus fervent for refrain.

All shapes and ages, women and men -
In all they numbered less than ten -
They comprised indomitable grain.

First time I've done this for fifteen years,
She said - to disbelief and cheers.
Inimitable, the voice was shy and pure.

Somehow it makes me think of sorrel,
A taste of sorrow, gently moral,
Lambent, telling lamentation's lure.

Pitying and dutiful,
The voice was very beautiful -
The pathos of a rosy smile, mature.

BONFIRE SOCIETY

Asked if I might
Have plans tonight,
I pause - the exchange is curbed.
Naming a town,
I catch my frown.
The barber looks disturbed.

I think of when,
Aged five, or ten,
This word was frankly feared.
Ever the same:
The way the name
Is annually revered.

Lewes - god,
It sounds so odd -
The hint of revolution.
Still it's the site
For bonfire night -
Mad passion's contribution.

Unlikely groups -
Resplendent troupes -
In alleys off the hill
Move dark en bloc
At six o'clock.
The mood is like Seville.

The crowds that pack
Like bric-a-brac
Around the war memorial
Contain all sorts -
Confused cohorts
That form two banks corporeal.

Fire is whiffed
From a stately drift:
The torch lights, tall and gentle,
Loom towards
The growing hordes.
The effect is elemental.

Comic and solemn
The woven column
Of high flames hot and swerving,
Rocks like a boat
And chokes the throat,
Sombre and unnerving.

The ceremony
Has a quality
That only remembrance has.
When they turn round,
They break into sound.
It's firebrand razzmatazz.

And on it goes -
Seven hours of shows
By pyromaniacs -
The bangers incessant,
Sky incandescent -
Police appear blasé and lax.

The barrels are trundled,
The effigies bundled
And blown up with deafening force.
The mobs, unloosed
Converge, reduced.
The finale is shambling and coarse.

How can it be?
- This anarchy
Anciently orchestrated -
That the role of a clown
By a county town
Has not been adulterated.

Watching these scenes,
A man from New Orleans
Regards each smoke-screened banner:
It's fierier by far
Than the glare of Mardi Gras;
It's a long way from Louisiana.

ADVENT IN THE MARDENS

Hammock-land - earthy and trenchant terrain - lags,
Shaking a hand of shaggier Hampshire. Nurtured
Through hundreds of years of insular handling, vistas
Grip with a strength and seriousness of mien.
Hiddenness confuses from a height.

Uppermost, the church's cream husk gives
In to timely dust-up grey. Hens, geese
Adhere to congregation. A cream woolly bull
Stands grisly, staunch. Houses hope, flint-spangled.
Darkness in the mud distils poor light.

Tarnished and tinny blue ramshackle
Shed - little brittle alloy in
A ring, on the hand pressing the palm
Or stroking the arm of Hampshire - pardoning
The scuttling of peasant Mardens' plight.

Wide-sweeping to the south, rough-rippled north,
The hammock-land, swiftly held, survives.
Come here - we contemplate, we long for lullabies,
We trudge and, wintry, stare into the past,
And lilt in land medieval, day as night.

GALE OVER OVINGDEAN

The sea, simultaneously gorgeous, grim,
Majestic, musical, charges blaring, as
The wind blows boisterous, wet and wild.
Rocked on our heels, we reel in the gale.
It lashes the ears. It lashes the eyes.
We marvel in isolation, inhaling
Flavours of the spray. We stand and
Stare. The air is open to a
Carnival sky, parades of cumulus
Water-cloud. Admiration
For the delicate dark grey rock
Formations is joy, sublime and raw -
After unhappiness. Fraught
From the prowl of pedantry,
We heave heavy sighs of satisfaction.
We champion chalk and pebble, both
Carried like talcum and talisman.
Buffeted by temperament
And fate, we are bettered
By a fearlessness of this our physics.
If it might not matter where
We were - well, this is where we are.
If time is of an essence,
We have taken place in time,
Examined by a tangible aggression.

A FROST IN FRISTON FOREST

A second night has left
A consecutive light ground frost.
In the forest's fringe of grass
Sheaves of stripes of blade
Are overturned to forms
Of spider or spiny starfish glass.

In the dawn sky the stars
Pall and fade as the sky
Attains all ice and cloudless blue.
The sun that was saffron when east
Of the sea is white in the later
Day, filtered into the woods.

The young beeches, green at the ground
Sway at the tops in the polar
Continental wind. The upper branches
Click, percussion - while
The wind unsettles the hard floor
Tartleted in brown beech leaves
Crunched and crackled underfoot.

It is meticulous, the hidden chip
And chisel of the wood life world.

BRIGHTON SEAFRONT LAMP STANDARDS

The dappled moon hovers, a cushion's outline
Over the row of lamps golden, divine,
Against an April evening sweet blue sky.

The day light seems almost to fight to the end
With a strength and a sadness the lamps help to lend.
The gulls glide, silent, slow and high.

At silver dawn in December or May
A lavender tincture starts the day.
The lamp light clearly decorates the air.

Risking reproach for performing aloof,
Suggesting a roofline bereft of a roof,
The lavender vanishes. Glass is all that's there.

Fronting an amethyst sunset: peach and
Apricot, succulent, sumptuous, grand -
The line is like a table lined with liqueurs.

The sea, moving full, is as heavily hard
As an army. The line stands a rock-steady guard.
Sustenance and vigilance endures.

The sun on a bright summer day seems to melt
The paint on the railings and lamp posts. What felt
So solid in the winter looks like clay.

The sun strikes the lanterns translucent, transformed
Briefly as whisky, chilled or warmed.
Their qualities exceed what words convey.

The threaded enchantment of lighting so styled
Extinguishes contrast of adult to child -
Daunted by design for such a flight.

Elegance troubled still never quite quails
But steadfast withstands torrents and gales -
Through rough rain like soon-dead sparklers white.

For winter the coloured cords, hanging between
The lanterns, live on in recession. They mean
More than any frittered neon sleaze.

Some promenade memories re-live the scene
When, thirty years back, the gold, red, green
And white bulbs scaled the poles and filled
                              Steine trees.

Ten different tiers of filigree
In aquamarine paint grow like a tree
From the black base, tapered in vanilla

Cream: and a cast iron crystallisation
Of the spirit of regency ornamentation -
Exquisite, catching the breath with every pillar.

In wafery grey the peaks are possessed
Of a strange and essentially English zest,
Shouldering allusions to the ruder -

When all the while the place has a flavour
Bold as the cold pastel sides of the Neva,
Grandiloquent as Danube views from Buda.

This is a stateliness lacking in menace,
Peerless by even the pavements in Venice -
Post-Victorian visionary cult.

Melon-glow shimmers from salt-filmed glass
In oriental frames - how can one pass,
And not be entranced, and not exult?

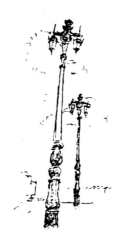

I see the word Sussex -
                it makes me feel good.
I'm really not sure
                that I think that it should.

A child observed the misty view.
"Why can't the sea be always blue?"
"Is there no satisfying you?"
- The child was only forty-two.

Where shall I find you, glum, funny film?
Somewhere where Wilmington men can wilm;
Somewhere eccentric with trees for glamour -
Where film buffs beam at The Moon And
                The Sledgehammer.

In the Walmer Castle the poets assemble.
My grandmother was born near this road.
Reading to these people, I try not to tremble,
Searching for sweet nature she showed.

I imagined a garden portrait,
        a swingchair, ear rings, hat.
Dear Lynda. I have these snowdrops,
        while recreating that.

MUSEUM: WEALD IN DOWNLAND

The winter day is damp and cold and raw.
The buildings, clean, discrete, are all of yore.

Some clustered, some alone are more remote -
Soft-surfaced, bright - surprising like a goat.

Their timber-framing patterns, mild and tight,
Lift thatch and tiles on wattled walls daubed white.

An open hearth's real ashes, aromatic,
Suggest a kind of welcome, warm, erratic.

Journeying into joineries we climb
Smooth spiral stairs of carpentry, sublime.

Three broad-backed healthy horses, dark and smart,
Are munching straw - more working works of art.

We cannot quite re-live by reconstruction,
Authenticating cultural induction.

Strange spectral dwelling place, the valley slope
Embodies conservators' toil and hope.

Pale lanes, of silver flint, and gold sand-stoned,
Encourage us to see our lives as loaned.

ELMS IN PRESTON PARK

The flakes fall thicker in the night
   And settle. After dawn,
The whitening of morning light
   Is more than once withdrawn.

The clouds of smoky grey return
   To colonise the sky,
And soon the snowfalls fill the air:
   The firm snow flakes look dry.

East winds come slicing. Flurries leap.
   White layers lie intact
Across the grass. White in some bark's
   Deep crevices is packed.

The clouds depart. The sun comes through.
   High up, the grey shoots redden.
Behind, pale blue the sky is lit -
   Then, later, it is leaden.

By noon the snow turns into rain.
   Old English elms in gloom
Stand grand. Their columns fork and crane
   And wedge in woody plume.

BEECH AT ERIDGE DEER PARK

A misreading of the maps
Resulted in a wrong turning.
Woodlet lobbies lined the fields' perimeter.

Across the clear blue sky
Shower clouds flew quickly,
Shedding beads rattling sweet leaves.

Down the steep dark bank,
Earthy, thin the path turned
Sharply, through a shaded opening.

From the dense foliage
A white-haired stranger's air of purpose
Walked, waved and called a mellow greeting.

Under a grand, solid
Beech we stood. I complained:
The biggest beech in Britain should be here.

I cited a reference.
His electronic compass took us
Through a gate into the deer park field.

There in fact it lay -
Choked and chopped, a heap of hollow
Light grey lifeless bark - felled on the grass.

RETURN TO WORTHING STARSEARCH

Our theatre tickets are as before.
Worthing is waiting. We are in awe,
Before we depart - before we disport
Ourselves as rabble plainly ought.
Monday comes. The die is cast -
Our pleasure hence to damn and blast.
Are we so wicked we cannot tell
We, mob dogs, bay at the boards of hell?
Or would we dare to tread that stage,
Confronted by such unseemly rage?
The first act, being a local band,
Receives a mildly miserable hand.
The guitarist, in a frock-coat jacket
Affects insouciance at the racket.
Into its infant howling now,
The rabble is ready for a row.
For some reason quite unclear
The judges receive a sporadic cheer.
Second on, from showbiz wearier,
A rotund man incites hysteria.
The language from the floor is foul.
Excruciated, people scowl.
Headbangers rise and wag their mops,
Hungry for their feast of flops.
Third comes a funereal man from Chester:
Ear-splitting screams from the collective jester.
An even older man appears
To sarcasm verging on genuine cheers.

A soft-shoe shuffler. A Worthing native.
The crowd turns docile, if creative.
A grey-haired black man, tinsel enigma,
Arranges flowers in a storm of stigma.
Excitement suggests that the building will shake
At the announcement of the interval break.

The lights go down for the second half.
The crowd erupts. They dance and laugh.
Next on stage, a skiffle group
Compete with a stripper: the skiffflers droop,
As the throng decides to sway,
Swinging inflatables. Swingers bray
And bleat and holler something rotten.
The skifflers themselves are fast forgotten.
A seventies elfin with afro hair
Struts like a parody of Leo Sayer.
A popular element within the revels
Puts on a side-show of pants-down devils.
At last, a woman takes the mike,
Wallowing in a mire of dislike.
The audience seriously sets to work.
The horns and klaxons go berserk.
The white-clad diva, prepared for a test,
Brings out the crowd's unholy best.
She seems to go on for quite some time
Dissembling oblivion to her crime.
Then there's a man singing Johnny B Goode -
Something that Worthing has understood.

He is from Brighton - not far away
But not sufficiently local today.
A trio, bathed in deep dry ice
Sing Tears For Fears - the irony nice.
Nice was never the word for this.
Most is boo and the rest is hiss.
Tedium tempers the body moronic;
Fatigue is a drama no less bionic.
All would be fevered all night long
With or without a stage or song.
Delilah has lost some discipline -
This year a syncopated din.
The curtain call of all the stars
Might as well have stood on Mars
To have any place but the utmost brave
In this ecstasy over talent's grave.
The winner is the elderly fred astaire -
His moment's applause unreal and rare.

Into the wind we all walk out,
Recovering from Worthing's clout,
Recovering from this year's outing -
Hoarse from bawling, shrieking, shouting.
Life will never seem the same
Should Worthing shut its halls of fame;
Life will be all bourgeoisie
When Worthing flunks its infamy -
However much we count the cost
In dignity that here we'd lost.

THE ARUN

The brooks trickle. Rivulets glissade.
Pastures, vales and meadows pattern
The bends. Bridges claw, recline or bathe.
Defunct, a canal accompanies, deformed.
Hamlets trail. Tidal towns garner. At
The final flattening, cobble and quoin
And Scandinavia speak through Roman
Trisantona's modern mouthpiece,
Harbourside.

WOOD FAIR AT BENTLEY

The borders of the fields are filled
With scores of white marquees. The skilled
Perform their spectacle of work,
While in the muddier copses lurk
Pulleys, hoists, construction, stoves
Darkly siphoning the droves.
Displayed among the tents and huts
Are juice and cider, plums and nuts,
Furniture, baskets, carvings and small
Owl-sounding wood-wind by which to call.

KINGLEY VALE YEW FOREST

Forming the shape of a U,
The forest falls over the downs,
Darkening deep autumn green.
Seen from a bridle path view,
Some sheep appear paler by crowns'
Confusion. We then intervene,
Approaching the base of the vale,
Into the blackish brown den.
Glassily flinted, the floors
Involve a meandering trail
Of roots. As if painted by pen
Or crayon - beneath the green gauze
Of poison, long branches, cracked, stray
In glossy self-polishing tan -
Red, green and buff - swing, twist, leap
From broad fluted boles. All delay
Alongwith arboreal span,
A germ, as the cups, ripe, red, seep.

FALLOW DEER IN ASHDOWN FOREST

Beneath and between the heaths a haze,
Blue, cheers the late autumn look.
Down from the stone pines, birch and gorse,
Among the oaks and pollard beeches
Delicate light is orange green.
Into a piece of hedge-side grass,
A young animal softly folds
All four limbs.

(In 1992, a large simple red sign spelling the words WEST PIER on the front of the former theatre building on the pier, facing the shore, was internally lit, suddenly creating a set of bright pink lettering, glowing in isolation over the night sea. The lighting, I am told, was funded by the South Eastern Electricity Board. - This monologue purports to express the thoughts of that lettering in stages over the subsequent eleven years.)

WEST PIER LETTERING

I

I am the ghost of the old west pier.
I emerge in the dark when the coast is clear.
For fifteen years my bones have lain
Creaking with crumbling flesh to feign
That promises can be fulfilled,
Under solemn threat of being killed.
As you rust you adjust to dilapidation:
A trial whose reward is this amputation.
It is hard to tell when to cry or laugh,
Your body already hacked in half.
I never expected eternal bliss
But I do want more from death than this.
I would give work to the workless and pay,
But I am insolvent, and curfewed by day.
So, nightly more skeletal, monochrome wreck:
I'll glow like some rubies at your neck -
Presiding over this interim -
Rose tinted token to shield the grim.

Clasped to the fabric, I have arrived
In time to pronounce what time deprived -
A peaceful surprise, alighting to lie
Like a silent busker in the low night sky.
I am no more, I should say, than a name,
Come here to comfort remains of my lame
Figure, to confront the taunt of ghost.
I advertise my broken host
By making good my guise as guest -
Literally manifest -
Gazing upon my crushed bisection,
Assigned to appear as pink confection.

II

Contingent, erratic and uncareered
I stayed. To second death I veered.
To me, so close to loss of hope,
Somebody ... somewhere ... threw a rope.
Now my light is back on course.
My light is like a Trojan force -
A transport crammed with rumination.
I ruminated on my station,
Fantasising phantoms vain
Which rumination set in train.
Being the ghost of the old west pier,
I worry now I am so near
To reincarnation. Should I survive,
Out of its depth my death may dive
Into a future of hope. My heart,

Salvaged, might from me depart.
I wonder if this is what I want:
New and computed - poor pink font.
Now I shall fade beside the cash
Refashioning me flush and flash.
My reputation rests on yearnings
I fear may overreach my earnings.
Pink, I have been subdued - a blush.
My white accessories point to a plush
Potential. What will become of me,
Reversed into bodily entity?
Nevertheless I am quick to concede,
This glory has yet to be guaranteed.
Strange, to find how death pans out -
In my case a matter of protracted doubt.

III

The pink withdraws, in phases fades,
Dimmed in the time delay pervades.
It seems a change is taking place -
The colour draining from my face.
Beloved allies flag when stunned,
Observing how the moribund,
Revived, is re-demoralised.
Was it my innocence people prized
More than my misery or my worth?
I entered this world not by birth
Of my body. I came later.
My body was always grander and greater.

We were a pair, my body and I,
Of purity. I now see why
Artists were drawn to this place to draw:
The meaning rich, the preening poor.
I am a ghost of a pier so old
Its ripe old youth seems oversold:
Finery in full proposed
Before the condition is diagnosed.
With each assaulting laden gust
I feel the rain enrich the rust.
Glories are farther from my grasp
Than fantasies. Great waves rasp
Against the iron's lurching dregs.
It is a trusting type who begs
For mercy from the venal realm.
My ten years' glimmer here at the helm
While gales blast by and waters heave
Show up the truth. I was naïve.

IV

Through the merry escapades
To, *quid pro quo*, the barricades,
I danced attendance, it could be said,
Into a dance of death. Twice dead,
I would not grieve for me alone
But for my person, skin and bone.
Had I my second time again
I might not say: cut short the pain:
Bluff my being whole and let

Ostentation flirt with debt -
But radical, since overdosed
With make-believe, being the ghost
Of the old but not the oldest
I could rescue by the boldest
Leap of faith some ancestry
And say to you: have done with me;
Have the nerve - much less renew -
For iron and wood, but sweet roofs too.
Light of my life, brave bashful tout,
Retire now from spelling it out.
Neither the ghost of the first west pier
Before the theatre and hall were here,
Nor the prefigurement of a style
Throughout that might seem infantile -
Was it a dream too meek, polite
To barter while a neophyte?
Meanwhile, unceremonious,
My role became erroneous.
My power disconnected, I
Retire as terminally shy.

V

The body's fame spread wider, faster,
Dramatised by each disaster.
No stage set could manufacture
Such a show of gradual fracture.
I was too simple ever to think
That flames might cause us all to sink.

My *mise en scène*, a backcloth burned,
Has lost the letters. Unconcerned
Since non-existent, having vanished
In company with woodwork banished
Into the rubble or sand below,
I am not myself. Although
Verse is written, words - trim shells -
Are hollow. No discourse dispels
The visible: a frame laid bare,
Unsigned - a sign of blank despair.
If they survived in any way
To be discovered, beached, astray,
A mighty size, my letters here
Would make a heavy souvenir.
I had supporters, admirers, friends;
But admiration cools - or ends.
Motives were many to pluck and plunder
Driftwood and debris when I went under.
Convinced the habitat was dead,
The starlings' vast formations fled,
As crowds of glum humanity
Laid to rest the vanity:
A legacy of wishing, slipped -
Profile slumped on sunken script.

ADAM ACIDOPHILUS

Adam Acidophilus
Attacks with his material -
Sardonic and hilarious -
The fake and the imperial.

The relish of audacity
Sparkles in his eyes.
He speaks with startling cogency,
Free to philosophise.

When Adam takes a microphone
To tell his calamitous fables,
The levity lays bare our lies,
And life is divested of labels.

DECEMBER IN CAMBER AND RYE

The Rother seems wide lying flat in the land,
    To lead amid waters alike.
Puffed on the clear horizon, a range
    Of cloud, lilac-silver, towers.
Sand has been driven to slide on the slabs
    Vaulting the grass-garnished dyke.
Left by the tempest, choppy grey-green,
    The sea, though relenting, still glowers.

Floppy-eared sheep on the short pale grass
    Graze, unremitting, voracious.
Light-weight on waters, gulls and swans
    And rallidae family swim.
East of the elder, thorn and gorse
    The marsh is moodily spacious:
Desolate structures - sheds and homes -
    Face wires forbidding and grim.

Back at the Camber sea shore,
    Remnants of rope in the sand
Tangle with seaweed and driftwood. Away
    On the dune the red flag flies.
Black weatherboard riverside warehouses prosper
    As, packed above the Strand,
Brick and tile, brown and bright orange, with white
    Sash windows are signally Rye's.

REVISION

The nuances of "attitude" seemed three-fold
        When first fitted
As title for the book. A so-called attitude
        To Sussex
Comprised approaches and reactions
        And accounts committed -
Expressing some identity in latitude
        To Sussex,
The term became less apt: in time, pretensions
        To the trendy
Instilled a note of self-regard and platitude.
        To Sussex
No self-styled attitudinising, glib *modus*
        Vivendi,
Could voice the deeper underlying gratitude
        To Sussex.